MINER'S POND

ALSO BY ANNE MICHAELS

The Weight of Oranges   *1986*

MINER'S POND

poems by Anne Michaels

M&S

CANADIAN CATALOGUING IN PUBLICATION DATA

Michaels, Anne, 1958-
   Miner's pond

Poems.
ISBN 0-7710-5855-1

I. Title.

PS8576.I24M56   1991   C811'.54   C90-095918-5
PR9199.3.M52M56   1991

The publisher makes grateful acknowledgement to the Ontario Arts Council for its financial assistance.

Set in Aldus by The Typeworks, Vancouver
Printed and bound in Canada by John Deyell Company

McClelland & Stewart Inc.
The Canadian Publishers
481 University Avenue
Toronto, Ontario M5G 2E9

For Martin, Arlen, and Howard Michaels

CONTENTS

I

MINER'S POND

in memory of Elie David Michaels

1

A caver under stalactites,
the moon searches the stars.

In the low field, pools turn to stone.
Starlight scratches the pond,
penetrates in white threads;
in a quick breath, it fogs into ice.
A lava of fish murmurs the tightening film.

The crow is darkness's calculation;
all absence in that black moment's ragged span.

.

Above Miner's Pond, geese break out of the sky's
pale shell. They speak non-stop, amazed
they've returned from the stars,
hundreds of miles to describe.

It's not that they're wild, but
their will is the same as desire.
The sky peels back under their blade.

Like a train trestle, something in us rattles.
All November, under their passing.

.

Necks stiff as compass needles,
skeletons filled with air;

osmosis of emptiness, the space in them
equals space.

Their flight is a stria, a certainty;
sexual, one prolonged
reflex.

Cold lacquering speed, feathers oiled by wind,
surface of complete transfluency.
The sky rides with tremors in the night's milky grain.

    •

Windows freeze over like shallow ponds,
hexagonally blooming.
The last syrup of light boils out from under the lid
of clouds; sky the colour of tarnish.
Like paperweights, cows hold down the horizon.

Even in a place you know intimately,
each night's darkness is different.

They aren't calling down to us.
We're nothing to them, unfortunates
in our heaviness.
We watch at the edge of words.

At Miner's Pond we use the past
to pull ourselves forward; rowing.

2

It was the tambourine that pushed my father
over the edge in 1962. His patience
a unit of time we never learned to measure.
The threat to "drive into a post"

was a landmark we recognized and raced towards
with delirious intent,
challenging the sound barrier of the car roof.

We were wild with stories we were living.
The front seat was another time zone
in which my parents were imprisoned, and from which
we offered to rescue them, again and again.

That day we went too far.
They left us at the side of the road
above St. Mary's quarry. My mother insists
it was my father's idea, she never wanted to drive away,
but in retrospect, I don't believe her.

This was no penalty; drilled in wilderness protocol,
happy as scouts, my brothers
planned food and shelter.
The youngest, I knew they'd come back for us,
but wasn't sure.

Hot August, trees above the quarry like green flames,
dry grass sharpened by the heat, and
dusty yellow soil "dry as mummy skin,"
a description meant to torment me.

They were rockhounds howling in the plastic light
melting over fossil hills;
at home among eras.

It was fifteen minutes, maybe less,
and as punishment, useless.
But the afternoon of the quarry lives on,
a geological glimpse;
my first grasp of time,
not continuous present.

•

Their language took apart landscapes,
stories of sastrugi and sandstreams,
shelves and rain shadow.
Atoms vibrating to solids,
waves into colours. Everything stone
began to swirl. Did the land sink
or the sea rise? When my brothers told me
I'd never seen the stars, that light's too slow,
that looking up is looking back,
there was no holding on. Beyond my tilting room
night swarmed with forest eyes and flying rats,
insects that look like branches, reptiles like rocks.
Words like solfatara, solfatara,
slipping me down like terraced water, into sleep.

  •

Full of worlds they couldn't keep to themselves,
my brothers were deviant programmers of nightmares.
Descriptions of families *just like ours*,
with tongues petrified and forks welded to their teeth,
who'd sat down to Sunday dinner
and were flooded by molten rock;
explorers gnawing on boots in the world's dark attic;
Stadacona's sons, lured onto Cartier's ship and held hostage,
never to see home again.

When the lights were out
my free will disappeared.
Eyes dry with terror, I plummeted
to the limbo of tormented sisters, that global sorority
with chapters in every quiet neighbourhood, linked by fear
of volcanic explosions and frostbite, polar darkness,
and kidnapping by Frenchmen.

  •

The ritual walk to the bakery, Fridays
before supper. Guided by my eldest brother
through streets made unfamiliar by twilight,
a decade between us.
I learned about invisibility:
the sudden disappearance of Röntgen's skin –
his hand gone to bones – and the discovery of X-rays.
Pasteur's germs, milk souring on the doorsteps of Arbois,
and microbe-laden wine – "what kind of wine?" –
the word "microbe"
rolling in my brother's 14-year-old mouth
like an outstanding beaujolais.
On these walks, frogs came back to life with electricity.
Sheep were cured of sheep-sickness.
Father Time, Einstein, never wore a watch.
Galileo saw the smooth face of the moon
instantly grow old,
more beautiful for being the truth.
The Curies found what they'd been looking for
only after giving up; they opened the lab and saw the glow,
incorruptible residue, radiant stain!

In winter, Glenholme Avenue was already dark,
with glass trees, elms shivering in their ice-sleeves.
As we walked, the essence of fresh bread
whirled into the secular air,
the street hungry for its pure smell.

Even now, I wrap what's most fragile
in the long gauze of science.
The more elusive the truth,
the more carefully it must be carried.

Remembering those walks,
I think of Darwin –
"no object in nature could avoid his loving recognition" –
on the bunk of the Beagle,

green with sea-sickness and the vertigo
of time. He was away five years
but the earth aged by millions.
Greeting him at Falmouth dock, his father cried:
"Why the shape of his head has changed!"
Stepping from cold night into the bright house,
I knew I'd been given privileged information,
because the excitement in my brother's voice
was exclusive to the street, temporary,
a spell.

         •

Brother love, like the old family boat
we call the tin can: dented, awkward,
but still able to slice the lake's pink skin.

         •

A family is a study in plate-tectonics, flow-folding.
Something inside shifts; suddenly we're closer or apart.

There are things brothers and sisters know —
the kind of details a spy uses
to prove his identity —
fears that slide through childhood's long grass,
things that dart out later; and pleasures like toucans,
their brightness weighing down the boughs.

Who but a brother calls from another hemisphere
to read a passage describing the strange
blip in evolution, when reptiles looked like
"alligator-covered coffee tables,"
evolution's teenagers, with a "severe case of the jimjams
during the therapsid heyday" —
remembering those were the creatures we loved best,
with bulky limbs and backs like sails.

Memory is cumulative selection.
It's an undersea cable connecting one continent
to another,
electric in the black brine of distance.

3

Migrating underground, miles below the path of the geese,
currents and pale gases
stray like ghosts through walls of rock.
Above and below, the way is known;
but here, we're blind.

The earth means something different now.
It never heals, upturned constantly.

Now stones have different names.

Now there's a darkness like the lakes of the moon;
you don't have to be close to see it.

.

My brother's son lived
one fall, one spring.

We're pushed outside, towards open fields,
by the feeling he's trying to find us.

Overhead the geese are a line,
a moving scar. Wavering
like a strand of pollen on the surface of a pond.
Like them, we carry each year in our bodies.
Our blood is time.

II

SUBLIMATION

Since the day he followed me into the train station,
uniform under his coat,
I've had no language.

Stuttgart to Paris in your car,
no belongings or papers
just the words inside;
useless in France,
meaningless in America.

I've written nothing without your help.

For twenty years you've been my shadow bride,
calling me back to myself.
In every city of my escape
I've heard your voice.
In Paris we spoke our mother tongue
in each other's arms.
You wept for the familiar sounds.

When I was 43 and met you for the first time
in Berlin, you cut my life in two.
I began again.
Today I'm 68 years old on the docks of New York,
gulls swerving and wailing
above our broken faces.
We say goodbye for the first time.

Once you called at midnight
to talk about Hindemith,
to tell me how his overtones connect each bar,
invisible thread, sounds we can't hear.
These harmonics guide us through the music, resolve

the twelve tones like mist in a valley,
the reflection of sky in water,
the illusion that what's unnamed remains unformed.
Our voices connected by black wire,
words carried on waves.

We are the strain and stress of a line,
the poem's tension singing in each black wire
of words, and between the first line and the last.
We are the angle of light that burns water,
the point of intersection that creates perspective.

You have lived Brecht's parable of the Chalk Circle.
When I was caught in the middle, you let go
so I wouldn't be torn to pieces.
Your actions have taught me what it is to love –
that it's holding back, as well as holding.

For the first time I'm going
where you can't join me. I know that home
is the one place you won't come.
But you of all people must understand –
the need to hear my language in every mouth.
I can't think in America.

I've never let myself describe you
and now that there's no time left
your meaning spills out of me
like the essence of an atom cracking
on the edge of speed's bowl,
liquid in its longing to become part of something else,
transformed.

Flesh moves to become spirit.

You were the only one to understand my conversion.
Many people have asked me about God;

my proof is manifestation,
that God can be called
"getting over fear."

I wanted badly that truth be a single thing;
now I know it won't be measured.
It wasn't Heisenberg or Hindemith, but you
who convinced me
that nothing can be unravelled to its core,
that truth is a field, a cage, a cloud of sound.
How else to reconcile the faces of those running away
with the faces of those turning away,
with the faces of those in uniform − that hair-shirt
that says more about a man than his eyes
because you can't tell the parts of his face
that are his.
How else to encompass both that crying and those
orders; the sound of my own voice
begging, and my voice telling jokes to the man
without shoes beside me on a train;
how else to encompass the moon's chilling scream
as it calls out in its bad sleep above the earth
and your voice on the phone,
waking me in Paris, Los Angeles, New York.

How else to reconcile you
with my family;
our knowledge of each other
an invisible hypotenuse
connecting your marriage and mine.

You are like the church bells in Heidelberg:
walking through Philosopher's Way,
no sound of the city passes through the wall of trees
except the intermittent bells
calling me back to the place.

I've woken many nights
sweating from the same dream,
my body sprouting hands,
ripping from my sides with the pain
of broken bone parting skin.

Last night I looked out
to the grocer's across your street,
baskets of flowers lining the sidewalk,
trembling in the dark wind.
The gasp of paper and leaves
made me 18 again –
nothing about the feeling had changed,
the ambush of longing October calls out.
I'm living proof
we don't stop wanting
what we can't have.

New York's a bad place to say goodbye,
but you're right –
it's no worse than any other.

For over twenty years
we've been joined: magician's hoops
caught and free, held together and apart
in desire and idea.

Like loons we travel underwater
great distances, to surface next to each other.
We burst up from water to air
to drift beside the serrated horizon of firs.

No matter where you are
or who you're near,
we come up for air together.

No matter my pace or distance,
it's you I surface to.

A LESSON FROM THE EARTH

*"God . . . began to play the game of signatures, signing His likeness
on to the world; therefore I chance to think that all nature and the
graceful sky are symbolized in the art of geometry."*

"Mine is the task of the mathematician."

— Johannes Kepler

I begged scraps from the Rudolphine Table —
the rinds of orbits, stars scattering like pips spat
from Tycho's chewing mouth.
His servants hovered the meal, poured wine
into everyone's glass
but mine. I was angrier than an incomplete equation!
Until Tycho gave me Mars. A feast
of numbers. Starved so long,
my eyes were bigger than my belly;
I'll have the answer in eight days, I cried,
leaning into my plate. But it took eight years
to lick it, clean.

We were sent to each other, Tycho and I;
nothing is casually
causal: all motion the result of invisible force.
We were sent for a reason,
like curtains blown in from an open window
to knock over a cup.
Everything fell.
Even the beloved circles of planetary paths
spiralled down,
empty as a swirl of apple skin.

My Martian obsession: I was a dog
prowling the dark, stars stuck in my fur like burrs.

Tycho's house was a box of noise,
numbers shook in my head like seeds in a melon.
No escape from the stamping and shouting
of masons and cooks, the hunters home with dinner,
and above all, Tycho's interfering howls.
So I worked at night, straining to hear
the sacred chant of geometric love!
I sharpened my compasses on the window ledge
and felt the breeze of planets in their nightly procession;
all night I tramped the sky, wearied by gravity,
tidal forces pulled my hair! Naturally,
I slept in. At lunch
there was a sneer under Tycho's moustache,
a look to remind me he'd stayed up late
every night of his life. Tycho,
who'd even fought a duel in the dark
and forever after rubbed metal polish
where his nose used to be. Every servant had a joke
about tarnished cutlery.
A true nobleman, Tycho smelled of silver.
Sometimes, during the day, I hid outside,
my favourite place behind a pile of broken dishes
that seemed always shiny with blisters of rain;
or else any place quiet enough
for the effort of turning chaos
into cosmos.

Prague crumbled around us.
The Church turned its children against each other,
set fires in its own house.
Over the city smoke hung purple, ripped with sunlight;
ravens sewed up the sky with their black stitches.
An 11-year-old girl prophesied the end of the world –
we had every reason to believe her.
Wounded shapes leaned against walls;
daughters and sons slipped between cannons and
through the fumes, to steal horse meat from the mud.

Amid all this – the problem
of Mars, god of war.
In the early hours I believed
only when I'd found the pattern of its orbit,
the hidden sense of it,
would the horrors end.

Priests point to sparrows, to rain,
to fruit falling from the trees,
in order to prove the earth stands still.
In the name of faith they only proclaim their doubt
by refusing to look through the telescope.
They say the truth is at stake; yes,
the truth seems nowhere else.
In Rome's Piazza dei Fiori
they burned Bruno, for believing in infinity.

We must learn at least this lesson from the earth,
that the greater must make room for the small,
just as the earth attracts even the smallest stone.
Just as the entire planetary system
rests on the plainest pattern.

As cathedrals replaced cross-beams and pillars
with a single arch,
so the Church must someday give up
hundreds of perfect circles,
for the simple, blasphemous ellipse.

In error begins truth.
I spent my life in dogged computation
to prove a sun-centred heaven. For years
my reasoning was a ball circling the curve of a hole,
but I believed I'd find an equation simple enough
to move the earth.
For twenty-two years I looked for ratios –
in sizes of the planets, in solar distances

and lengths of orbits – until God whispered:
measure not from the earth but from the sun.
And the heavens opened.

I know now why sailors sing.
The sea is so big it swallows geometry,
but not time.
Heaving and hauling with one voice,
they shift the sky on their backs.
So it is with the planets; dancing,
their skirts flare out behind them –
equal areas in equal time –
harmony of the spheres.

I used to think we escape time
by disappearing into beauty.
Now I see it's the opposite.
Beauty reveals time.

I saw my first eclipse when I was nine, above Emmendingen,
the moon rising from the clouds like an infant's head
in its web of blood; the last time
I held my father's hand.

Everything human and broken
depends on perfection.

Imperfect man, left unfinished
with the purpose of becoming whole.

A prisoner moon, I'm caught between papal earth and
Lutheran sun, heretic to both.
I've been pushed from Tubingen, Graz and Prague.
In Linz they took away my books
until Paul Guldin got them back –
he may be a Jesuit, but first
he's a mathematician.

They asked for me in every town; they'd be happy
with even false confession.

From Linz we travelled up river
until the Danube froze, and I had to leave
Susannah and my daughters in Regensberg.
My head banged like a turnip against the back of the wagon
all the way to Ulm. But in my arms
the only copy of the Rudolphine Tables,
including a map of the world, a chronology of history, and
the positions of one thousand,
one hundred, and thirty-six stars.
Two lifetimes of devotion,
one spent bent over paper,
the other – Tycho alone in the dark,
his face red from leaning back, hand in his pocket
around a fist-sized globe of the sky
he carried with him since he was a boy.

Now Tycho's gone. His instruments –
the finest, none to match them anywhere –
rust in Tengnagel's cellar.
Gone, Tycho's Castle of the Stars,
the printing press and paper mill,
his forest, fish ponds and flower gardens,
his compass-makers and measurement-takers.

And Emperor Rudolph – gone;
with his imperial library and mechanical treasures,
the singing fountains and glass orchestras.

Tonight, arriving in Ulm,
I remembered a night as cold as this,
years ago, when the recognizable sky saved me
from the unrecognizable world.
From a bridge over the Moldau, all mystery poured up
and complex Prague fell away.

The sudden gift of the comet –
like a word mouthed, a sign,
a rock thrown across a lake without a sound –
and looking down, I saw the whole sky floating in the river:
"as above; so below."

Looking up again, I saw what has always been,
suspended since time began, for anyone to discover –
God's eternal clue:
the moon in its wet skin of light,
the moon not less in its halfness.

What I learned then sustains me
through every sorrow:
it's the believer who keeps looking for proof.

MODERSOHN – BECKER

*"There are many degrees of power in the world, and nowhere is the
difference in degree greater than in the case of human will and
human desire, just as water boils at one temperature, and molten iron
at another."*

– Fyodor Dostoevsky

1

It did not free me to leave him.

All day at Worpswede rain stretches to the ground,
air like wood grain; burls of cloud.
Bark puckers on thin trees:
fingers too long in water.
By the end of the path, my sweater is beaded
with mist, a silver armour.
Where road wedges forest,
work horses stagger like body builders.
Snow is messy with spring, mud stains
under trees, like pools of shadow.
These are days when day doesn't arrive;
at night the same darkness falls into place.

I could smell pipe smoke in his hair.
Before I left,
in the peculiar quiet of a winter house,
windows startled dumb with ice –
we sat together on the stairs.
His head leaned on the banister.
Everyone said I was selfish.
Fear is selfish.

From Paris I wrote his name on a year of envelopes
until I finally saw

the shape of it: Otto – two bodies, two mouths.
The gutter ran with lights
and in the empty street I heard our loneliness
in a dog's throat.

Every way into myself
fills up with blood.

The joy that's close to terror; colour,
the hot pulse that hurts through veins.

In this light his eyes are clotted with oil.
The studio smells of wood smoke.
The birds ask their same questions.

My hands are stained with his face.

2

In 1900, Cézanne's paintings were stacked against a wall
in Vollard's basement. I couldn't believe
those secret squares of colour, fermenting in the dark,
unrecognized.
Paris wasn't the same after that.
And watching Rodin shape thought,
like a blind man learning a face,
I saw what it means to merge with work.
Rodin, who felt the sculptor Clara could become,
cut away the excess.
My friend emerged in his hands.

Watching him gather hair like flowing water
from a stone scalp,
pulling the face open
into love –
breasts like leaves dripping with rain,

legs taut as roots –
I suddenly understood that painting too
never lets you escape
awareness of the human hand:
the source of light
is the painter's body.

I thought that finding my own hot centre
would teach me colour.
Clara circled her clay while I stared so long at the canvas
I was dragged under.
Even the spirit has limits,
humility rising like silence,
the silence of light, gold rising from the fields.

●

We left Paris, the Pont des Arts
still lined with violets.
At Worpswede, the hills burned under September's glass.
Clara and I wore white to soak up the last light,
like bread the last bit of soup.

We first saw Rilke pushing furniture
through a doorway. I named the scene:
Struggle, With A Table;
later learned the truth of it.

By the fire, listening to a chamber concert,
the kind of music where loss wears gloves.
Rilke's eyes were on us.
That night he said things like "let me stay in the storm!"
and "give me autumn!"
Everyone was aware of him.

He followed me outside;
we washed our faces in the cold air.

●

What was missing in me, Rilke knew.

Nights together, midnight tea
in my studio, where, he said,
"everything becomes mysterious."

He talked about Tolstoy, and how we must earn
death. From Rilke you can learn about love
just watching him hold a cup or peel an orange.

Black roofs bled through thin snow,
words on a page. At the window, our legs
long against each other, grass in a current.

But his kind of love deepens
only with loss. He smells what's burning
better than what's fresh.
Rilke, don't be a "writer," stay
a man who writes!
"What do you know about it, Paula?"

That's how it was. To him, I was Paula.
But he was always "Rilke."

●

Skating on the Christmas pond;
lamps like owls in the trees.
I crushed fans of spruce and buried my face in my hands
as if in a book. While Rilke read inside,
his beautiful head bent from his body
like a stem "broken" by the line of water in a vase.

He married Clara and soon she was moving horizontally,
a figurehead on a ship, pregnant with their daughter.

His invisible barrier between them;
birds hitting glass.

                    •

Married, my aesthetic turned physical,
a knowledge I couldn't paint:
a heap of coltsfoot,
its yellow points curling on the table;
the white bedroom of birches, our faces cold,
the warmth of us under clothes – sometimes
chocolate, a blanket – until darkness
rolled on top of the light, leaving only
the small breathing spaces of stars.
The accidental beauty
of things brought in from outside,
leaves and crushed mignonettes carried in on sweaters:
the unplanned life that purled our days.
Following his trail: chair still rocking, lit pipe,
the apple changing colour on the plate.

Only love sees the familiar for the first time.

The light changing Otto's face, changing
him.
Winter turning the walls blue.
Imagining him naked, even as he stood there,
naked.

                    •

Opened by hills;
unnerving metal yellow of birch leaves
between my teeth;
forest's green chill on my shoulders.
Ice filled my veins,
the pond the colour of drowned ghosts, ragged as a shadow.

Trees pushed up through my throat,
leaves crowded my eyes and
I looked. Grateful, bursting with shape and colour.
I held my husband until I felt his face inside my own,
until my skin was blind with attention –
and still I didn't know anything, still
my hand was stupid.
My eyes went black, I held the brush,
choking on a thread of song.

.

I started again; where everything starts:
at the body. Classes in life-drawing,
training my hand to see.

In Paris alone,
my family waiting for me to give up
so I could go back to being "happy."

Every day, failure boiled up into my throat
and stayed there.

.

Obsession is the sacrifice of light
to the richness of submergence.
But love is separation,
the membrane of the orange dividing itself,
the surface of silver
that turns glass into a mirror.

There's failure in every choice.

Art emerges from silence;
silence, from one's place in the world.

·

Not that paint captures light,
but that light breaks free from the paint.

I imagined autumn in Worpswede, the tangled red
wire of empty bushes, a ceramic sky
crazed with branches. I sank deep in myself,
breathing in as if my bones were cedar.

Nowhere have I felt closer to love
than there, alone in that city.

Stars are flickering tips of snakes;
starlight, their fragile skin cast behind.

My dreams longed for Otto, for forest, for home.
I woke and the space was empty, except for paintings:
my step-daughter playing recorder,
hollow vowels slipping through the trees,
streaming behind her;
my sister's black hair pulled tight,
sleek as a mink, her braid a watery tail down her back.

Then I felt crazy – my two lives, simultaneous.

Two whites: snow on the birches.

·

Fulfillment is wordless,
the silence when skin takes over.

But when you're not speaking with skin,
you must love with language.
Rilke would say that's even more intimate –

the instant words become picture,
leaping from his throat, to my inner eye.

.

The first spring day, with Otto in the garden.

My mother crossed the grass, her arms open,
like a child waiting to be lifted.
Since five in the morning she'd travelled towards me.

We pulled the table out to the verandah,
set the blue dishes.
My dress round as the billowing cloth.

3

Branches dip, dripping.
Rain gets in everywhere, its animated shadow
fills every surface.
Dreams that usually evaporate in the light
stay wet with darkness.

That I'm looking for something I can't find
makes me strangely satisfied.
It fills me with time.

All my life I've been saying grace
for hunger: invisible, smelling of earth,
heavy as cattle down a darkening field,
their bodies pushing their heads close to the ground,
their necklaces of bells.

.

Every painting is a way of saying goodbye.

FLOWERS

There's another skin inside my skin
that gathers to your touch, a lake to the light;
that looses its memory, its lost language
into your tongue,
erasing me into newness.

Just when the body thinks it knows
the ways of knowing itself,
this second skin continues to answer.

In the street – cafe chairs abandoned
on terraces; market stalls emptied
of their solid light,
though pavement still breathes
summer grapes and peaches.
Like the light of anything that grows
from this newly-turned earth,
every tip of me gathers under your touch,
wind wrapping my dress around our legs,
your shirt twisting to flowers in my fists.

ANNIVERSARY

Tonight a Buick's our bedroom,
cold wind off the lake muffled by closed windows.
Thirty years ago we drove through dark mountains
on a narrow road, as if under blankets with a flashlight.
Three days and two nights to the sea,
past grain elevators leaning against the horizon
like the heads on Easter Island;
under stars like ibises
swooping through mangroves.
Thirty years from our wedding and still
we're sleeping in cars. Still
awake as the moon, foreheads burning.

FRESH MINT

Fresh mint slinks towards us through the dark kitchen,
crowds the table,
loud with its own good suggestions.

Persuasive as an extra electron, it changes
conversation, reminds us of
something. Insidious.
The way there's always
more glasses than guests at the end of a meal.

It binds us in its loose weave,
thread of moonlight in water.

Soon we don't notice
the wild smell,
being so filled with it.

PHANTOM LIMBS

"The face of the city changes more quickly, alas! than the mortal heart."

— Charles Baudelaire

So much of the city
is our bodies. Places in us
old light still slants through to.
Places that no longer exist but are full of feeling,
like phantom limbs.

Even the city carries ruins in its heart.
Longs to be touched in places
only it remembers.

Through the yellow hooves
of the ginkgo, parchment light;
in that apartment where I first
touched your shoulders under your sweater,
that October afternoon you left keys
in the fridge, milk on the table.
The yard — our moonlight motel —
where we slept summer's hottest nights,
on grass so cold it felt wet.
Behind us, freight trains crossed the city,
a steel banner, a noisy wall.
Now the hollow diad
floats behind glass
in office towers also haunted
by our voices.

Few buildings, few lives
are built so well
even their ruins are beautiful.
But we loved the abandoned distillery:

stone floors cracking under empty vats,
wooden floors half rotted into dirt;
stairs leading nowhere; high rooms
run through with swords of dusty light.
A place the rain still loved, its silver paint
on rusted things that had stopped moving it seemed, for us.
Closed rooms open only to weather,
pungent with soot and molasses,
scent-stung. A place
where everything too big to take apart
had been left behind.

At Katimbang, dead birds rained out of the sky.
Statues walked.

Whole forests – strewn like driftwood.
Tides so fast, fish were stranded,
then picked from the ground like a crop.

Father, I remember when we first
sailed through together –
how simple fear was, then.
Docked at Merak you told the story
of Sunda ghost, a sailor
who paid for the sins of this life
in the next, by having to gather
all the islands in the Strait.
The lights of port behind you;
breeze snapping the ropes:
"at night you'll hear him howling,
his hands full and his work half done."
My hair jumped when I first heard the sound.
You kept me scared. Then told me
about orang-utans, who'll howl like babies
when the weather's shifting.
Now I can tell you,
Sunda Strait is surely haunted.

Our destination was Hong Kong,
carrying cargo from Belfast.
As usual, the first day we pull from shore,
each man was busy with his own thoughts.
And as usual, Willy – John's son – was below,
sleeping off his leave;
he never came aboard on his own legs.

At first it sounded like cannon fire, a distress;
but not a ship in sight.
The threat of damnation isn't always
something you can see.
Then a line of weather covered half the sky.
I shortened sail, turned south-west to face the wind.

Like meteors, like white comets chained with flame,
the pumice fell – stones bigger than a man's head,
the size of pumpkins –
then smaller ones, almost worse
because they came so fast; in seconds
we were deep in ash.

The sea was a swaying field of pumice,
frozen foam.
And then – a jungle floated towards us,
palms standing straight up;
as if we sailed through dry land.

Midnight, suffocating
on a sea that looked like dirty ice.
Choked with sulphur,
eyes burning into our heads.
Cinders everywhere; the air itself was on fire.
The sea boiled.
Father, at thirty fathoms,
the lead came up hot!
Mastheads and yardarms – lined with spark.

By morning, the strait was clear.
We even laughed when Willy,
who'd slept through it all,
came up for watch and wouldn't believe a word.

But then we saw the lighthouse at Fourth Point
snap like a stem.

And day was night,
land was sea,
the earth fell out of the sky.

Noon, and we were in a darkness you could feel.
Burning mud, glowing green and blue,
slapped the deck –
the sound that hits a coffin.
We shouted constantly, because we couldn't see;
and dug, for fear of sinking under the weight.
I called for the sidelights
and sent the two James's forward.
The mate and second in either quarter,
and someone to keep mud off the binnacle glass –
though we were blind as the dead.

Lightning lit our faces,
ugly with work.
The air – smeared solid.

When it stopped
we fell where we stood, as if we'd had only
the exact amount of strength.

The dark was full of stories,
of names of wives and children;
stories that, when light returned,
would never be spoken again.

It lightened enough to see the horizon.
Our first sight of land was West Island.

A mist of sand began to fall.
Krakatoa roared, ear-aching loud,
though we were a full seventy-five miles away.
The *Charles Bal* – from truck to waterline,
spars, sails, and ropes –

hard with mud;
as if she'd been raised from the bottom.

A miracle, not a man hurt.
But – in Anjer, Merak,
all the villages of the Java Coast!

Father, the places you stopped so often
for water and wood, meat and fruit
have vanished.

They say that when the blast came,
in the streets of Katimbang
mud galloped fast as horses;
that burning ash pushed through floors
like pillows bursting their stuffing.
They say that when people ran through the streets
they left red footprints of fire.
That their bare arms looked like torn sleeves.

We knew them.

They say that even now, even far as Ceylon,
when you cut open fish
you find jewellery that belonged to the dead.

The town of Tjiringin is now ocean.

BLUE VIGOUR

I think, if you have lived through a war
or have made your home in a country
not your own, or if you've learned
to love one man,
then your life is a story.

Eight thousand feet above the sea's devotions
sail the four Ngong hills.
The East Wind – "King Solomon's favourite horse" –
rides over the plain to the foothills;
you follow the monsoon's path to my farm,
desert in your clothes and hair.

If you love a man who's not your husband,
your life becomes the story everyone else tells.

For months we were still as animals
alert to an enemy. We stalked each other with the charged
passivity of the inevitable.
With the patience and impatience of obsession.

I learned about you
the way I learned about the river
at the edge of my farm –
I can't see it from the house,
but know its path by the acacias
that grow along it.

What I couldn't foresee
led me to you.

During the act of greatest trust
my husband gave me a lasting gift.

I was rotten with his *mal d'amour;*
they had to send me home.
Almost 30, back in my mother's house.
When I could walk again, her narrow arm
steered me through the garden,
green peony hands glistening
like the acres of coffee I'd left behind.
I leaned against her,
missing her youth as well as my own.
Home, yet not home.
Although the marriage was over,
I had the farm.
Although we hadn't yet touched,
I longed for Ngong and your body.

Sleepless on the boat
I pressed against the railing,
leaned into my future.
To deny another's happiness
by denying your own –
that could only be an adult misery.

I know your value
because you give yourself
just as you're leaving.
Each sojourn refines our feeling –
together we are stones tumbling to jewels,
beans polishing in the coffee-dryer,
gleaming under the lanterns.

When we stayed at your house
on the Takaunga, the moon was firm
in the shaking sky.
We were alive as coral pools,
where water shapes the rock
and rock shapes water.

Each time you return
you ask for another story.
Your expectation lets me love you
when you're gone.
My wanting would have both encased me
and driven me out of my skin
like an insect under the canopy at night —
were it not for words.
Each day I write to greet you.

Those mornings when one side of my bed
is cool with your absence,
I rise to the window and loving you,
the Ngong hills gather me in.

With each parting
my heart is forced to grow,
because the only way to love you
is to love each particle of green and
each animal part of life —
muscle, skin, and bone —
that dots and darts and hides
in the view from my room.

And now that you've learned to fly,
and really ride King Solomon's East Wind,
I have to love the air.

ON THE TERRACE

They say the brush is strapped to my hand –
it's not true.
My palms fold in and Gabrielle wraps them,
in powdered gauze, to stop the chafing.
In fact, the brush fits nicely in that crevice,
my fingers like vines around a trunk.
Sometimes it startles me;
my twisted joints, the brush so straight.

All morning, sweating over the olives –
those leaves use every colour for grey.
Years ago, when I stopped working outside –
what a commotion
because a man came in out of the rain.
Raphael didn't have to drag his canvas through fields
in order to paint sunlight.
I was tired; every time I looked up
the light was somewhere else.
Clouds, the wind, made a sleeve change colour or
leaves turn over their other green.
It's lonely, letting the world wash over you.
Those days, everyone looked away. In love;
or drinking, heads leaned back,
eyes focussed on the bottom of a glass.
But now I'm kept company.
Women look me in the eye when I take their clothes off.
I'm a fine son of a tailor, painting nudes!
Gabrielle gains twenty pounds under my brush.

When I was young, I wanted to move with the world,
didn't realize the world moves in us.
A still life isn't about fruit, but about
time.

And there's a stillness inside things
as they move; think of waterlilies –
Poor Monet, his blind eyes filled with water!
The lilies float in his mind.

That's why I can't agree with Zola –
so concerned to describe the surface,
he forgets the spaces between things,
forgets that touching isn't holding.
Too busy with "iridescence" and "shimmering,"
he forgets to say it's raining.
It was my mistake too, forgetting space.
When I was a student of the Seine
with Monet at Bougival,
we learned how colours vibrate.
But space vibrates too.
That's what musicians know.
If Zola were here, he'd sit in that chair,
eyes burning everything in sight –
convinced that's the way to see –
and in the end, like all the others,
he'd deduce:
the brush is strapped to my hand.

Stillness in motion. I illustrate my point.
They carry me like a king from one room to another;
when I shout,
they rush to pick the brush hairs from the paint.

And now that I have no hands,
I long for clay.
Why begin sculpture now?
Riviere's the only one who'd ask.
I couldn't tell him
it was because of a dream,
that I'd slept back, thirty years,
to *The Bathers* at Versailles.

Girardon himself had become limestone;
he looked so happy there, among them.
Now I want a woman
who'll wait for me in a garden,
in any weather, every light.

In the afternoons I watch them work the stone.
One day, without lifting a hand,
the form in my head
will be exactly what I see.

STONE

Beatrice called him a pig and a pearl.
But she also liked to say,
lovers are equal only when so steeped
in corruption, knowledge of the other
is no longer a weapon.

Modi was a fallen king,
royalty in trousers held up with rope,
quoting Dante and Petrarch on park benches.
Cocaine and absinthe made him
play the naked bull in the street.
I've heard all the stories from everyone
who never knew him.
Modi wandering the halls, ripping wallpaper,
gouging at plaster until his nails bled –
because he was drunk. No. Because
he wanted to get at brick,
to feel stone under his fingers.
At night he used to steal
blocks from construction sites, until
the war, when no one was building any more.
He resented his own walls,
hundreds of stone women surrounding him,
unreachable.

He was close to Rivera
and painted him as a balloon;
Diego will never get stuck, he said,
Diego's free.

His old self clung to him,
an open mouth on his sleeve; a shadow
that turned him around in the street,

or in his sleep. His last nights were spent
with a stranger, the Greek, who knew nothing
of his failures, but knew
the Mediterranean.
He drank himself back to where he was born.

There are two kinds of spiritual biography:
Modi stuffed his soul with life.
I starved for the sake of my soul.

At first it wasn't passion, felt more
like memory – as if, in remaining true to myself,
to everything in my life that had come before,
there could be no direction but towards him.

We even met in an old embrace.
Modi was alone in Nice,
months after we'd been introduced,
when suddenly he knew me.
He came back to Montmartre. For weeks
we walked the city, resting in a cinema
or crémerie and he never stopped talking.
His baroque attentions, his rococo tongue!
The whole city in his face.
We drank to his *cara Italia*, his mother,
to Giovanna who he'd never see grown;
but he stayed sober and no hashish,
which he used to take like dinner mints
after meals at Rosalie's or the Rotonde.

He accepted beauty wherever it was offered,
black iron fences against the snow,
bare trees smeared like charcoal on a wet sky.

We sat together at dozens of tables,
so poised for love, if I moved an inch
I would've caught one wing in the sea

and toppled, squawking, water-logged,
everything spoiled by closeness.
Faith turned to hunger
like a sweater pulled inside out, over my head.

Our walks transformed Paris: desire
clinging like windy paper to legs;
sharp as gasoline and leather polish, wet wool and
Modi's scent in my coat;
hopeless as the horses patrolling a vanished city,
pulling beans and potatoes in the crowded streets.

The higher the ledge of his art,
the more the world pulled at his feet.

It wasn't only his lungs not strong enough.
The last trip home, he showed photos of his heads.
His friends brayed and barked, begged him
to put the stone out of its misery,
to smash it back into pavement.
He spent months on a single carving.
Five or six years
of happiness, nights when he lit candles and
embraced the day's work, a pagan.
Later he endured the portraits abused too –
as a roof for rabbits, as walls for a chicken coop –
by Libion and the butcher who took them
in exchange for cheese and eggs.
Nobody tells that part of the story.
When he was dead and worth ten times his life,
of course they tried to sell them.
But the canvases were too damaged.

No one cares about Modi now, another painter
from an old avant garde,
a man whose faces have been cut
into postcards, puzzles, ashtrays.

Only limestone loved him perfectly,
resisted with integrity, showed him
what to do. Demanded slowness, will,
mistakes not easy to fix.
But paint submitted to frenzy.
He was powerful. His love
was less.

His great dream – to sculpt a temple of women,
the "pillars of tenderness" he believed
held up the world.
Instead – his nudes. Outside of time and place;
no fruit, no flowers or furniture,
just the glowing body,
the certainty of pleasure.
A scandal –
to paint the body no longer anonymous:
each woman with a different knowledge.
It was Picasso's work that was immoral –
he tore off the woman's clothes then
tore apart the woman.
Modi's models simply – disrobed.

He wasn't a cubist, because he believed
if you break the bowl you can't describe
what's in the bowl;
destroy a shape – its spirit dissipates.
He was only a cubist when it came to love.

His portaits – every face a eulogy to stone
but without its calm.
The concentration of a last glance or
an approach;
as if, as he held them in his gaze,
they were already melting away.
He believed it was better to burn with time,
to match its speed with your own,
like the moment you can follow rain with your eyes.

When he painted,
he found you.
Beatrice was fire, Jeanne was nectar,
I was clear water; affected by the slightest touch.
He focussed on my throat, that long river between
brain and body, between what you say and
what you give. The line of my neck
graceful, elegant as the handle of a pitcher.
My face flushed under its whiteness,
so covered with his touch, yet
so untouched, so – tragic!

Jeanne looked like a gypsy, with her violin.
But all she knew was Bach.
Her devotion was a fugue,
he got tangled up in himself, trying to leave her.
He did everything to push her away;
she did nothing but remain still.

He judged her gently,
painted every weakness, her double chin,
but the whole story came out on canvas,
everything she was thinking:
how Modi looked at four in the morning,
how he slept, close, without forgetting her.
Jeanne was a woman who could look at one face forever,
if she knew how the arms held.

When he died, she jumped,
big with Modi's life.
I feel certain it was a son.

No one believed in him, not even Jeanne,
who in the end, believed only in his body.

A few years ago
on a train to London, a man

brought Modi back to me.
He was Welsh and lived in a place so set aside
it was like the detail of a painting.
I liked him right away; when he sat down he said,
pardon me if I smell of horses.
He'd walked through fields to reach the station.

Half his life in Africa, and now
he spent his days drawing farm animals
in a motel room by the sea.
We talked our way across England;
he said, I belong nowhere, half here,
half there.
I'd give anything to see this place
as I used to – when I was young.
When my life was still imagined.

We passed fields smoky with rain,
hay lying loose, flat as wet hair.
The glass was ghostly bark, wrinkled with water
and it was like looking out a cafe window –
I'm an old woman but I could smell wet wool,
horses, the sweet brown breath of coffee.

The Welshman said,
some people regret not what they've done
but what they haven't, and then decide:
this is my life. No;
you've missed your life.
But even the truth can't change the past.
When you're old, time is like a toothache,
still –
you're happy to have teeth in your mouth.
Pardon me if I've upset you.

Better to let the past dissolve in you,
grow small; still as
smell.

I love horses, the man said,
they're the most noble of animals.
They're beautiful even while they're working.
It's the *Iliad*, isn't it –
where even the horses weep on the bloody field.

It was cold, late afternoon, the room was dark –
Paris winter – but the window
was a painting, thick with light.
Modi's arms around my waist.
He told me that in Cagnes
the light was so bright it drove him crazy,
so he and Soutine stepped into a barn;
it was cool and dark
and suddenly he felt the warm
breath of a horse on his hair.

Our gratitudes were heaped against the day.
In the dimness, the room was a garden,
silk waterfalls of robes down the closet door and
flowing from sill to floor.

Keep everything you can't.

III

WHAT THE LIGHT TEACHES

"I break open stars and find nothing and again nothing, and then a
word in a foreign tongue."

— Elisabeth Borcher

1

Countless times this river has been bruised by our bodies;
liquid fossils of light.

We shed our ghost skins in the current;
then climb the bank, heavy and human.

The river is a loose tongue,
a folk song. At night we go down to listen.
Stars like sparks from a bonfire.
We take off what we are,
and step into the moon.

2

When there are no places left for us,
this is where we'll still meet.
Past the white fountain of birches,
green helmets of willows.
Past the boulder that fastens the field
like a button on a pocket.
Here, where trees you planted are now twice our height.

In winter we'll haunt your kitchen, our love
an overturned bowl, a circling lid.
We'll visit the creaking bog with its sunken masts;
fly over a death mask of snow
and the frozen pond striped with grass —

to our river, humming between closed lips.
Attentive as your favorite poet,
Tsvetaeva — who listened with the roots of her hair.

3

Birds plunge their cries like needles
into the thick arm of afternoon.

Beyond the closed window, soundless pines —
a heavy green brocade; and the glowing, stiff
brush cut of the corn.
Wands of wild calla.
Lilies tall as children.

You're asleep on the couch, head up, as if in a bath;
summer heat turns thin white sleeves
pink against your skin.
Sleeping as if you'd waited years
for a place to close your eyes.

Everything familiar:
dishes and smells, faces in oval wooden frames,
tins of Russian tea
with their forest scenes, their borders of black and gold,
lining the shelves.

We float in death,
the ordinary world holds together
like the surface tension of water,
still and stretched, a splash of light.
The shadow pattern of leaves,
a moving tattoo on your bare legs.

4

Sometimes I was afraid to touch him,
afraid my hand would go right through him.
But he was alive, in a history
made more painful by love.

I prayed to the sky to lift our father's head,
to deliver him from memory.

I wished he could lie down
in music he knew intimately, and become
sound, his brain flooded by melody so powerful
it would stretch molecules, dismantle thought.

5

Suspended in flux, in contortions of disorder,
in the frozen acrobatics of folding and faults,
the earth mourns itself.
Continents torn in half and turned into coastlines,
call for themselves across the sea.
Caves, frantic for air, pull themselves up
by the ground, fields collapsing into empty sockets.
Everywhere the past juts into the present;
mountains burst from one era to another,
or crumple up millennia, time joining at its ends.

We also pleat time.
Remembering, we learn to forget.
The kind of forgetting that stops us, one foot
in the spring soil of your farm,
the other in mud where bits of bone and teeth
are still suspended, a white alphabet.
The kind of forgetting that changes
moonlight on the river into shreds of skin.

The forgetting that is the heart's
filthy drain,
so fear won't overflow its deep basin.

Even in its own confusion,
in its upheavals and depressions,
the earth has room in its heart.
Carefully, part by part, it replaces us.
Gently, so bones may embrace a little longer,
mud replaces marrow.

The dogs slip like mercury through the long grass.

How can we but feel they're here,
in the strange darkness of a thermosensitive sky,
even as light gushes over rocks
and the sun drips sweet fat the colour of peaches
over fields. Here, in the noise of the river,
a mother gives birth in a sewer;
soldiers push sand down a boy's throat.

Theirs are voices we hear
but can't hear, like the silence
of parents rounded up in a town square,
who stopped their tongues in time,
saving children by not calling them in the street.

Our father's daughters, we can't dream ourselves
into another world, see things differently.
Instead, we try to withstand memory
with memory, to go back further, to before:
back to the dacha in the high forests of Kochtobel,
to the Moyka in our mother's silvery photo of Petersburg,
to the wooden sidewalks of Kiev.
You read poems in the old language
even our parents can't speak –

what we save, saves us —
and in your mouth the soft buzzes are natural as cicadas,
the long "ayas" like bird calls.

Language is how ghosts enter the world.
They twist into awkward positions
to squeeze through the black spaces.
The dead read backwards,
as in a mirror. They gather
in the white field and look up,
waiting for someone
to write their names.

Language remembers.
Out of obscurity, a word takes its place
in history. Even a word so simple
it's translatable: number. Oven.

Because all change is permanent,
we need words to raise ourselves
to new meaning: tea and dacha and river.

6

It stopped me, the first time
I looked out at our father in the yard and saw
how she leaned her head on his shoulder —
familiar, and full of desire.

Together they looked at a nest in the bushes,
inspected strawberries.
Although the air was humid with lilacs,
heavy with insects and rain,
she was cool in a dress the colour of the moon.

You were reading by the open door.
The sound of a lawn mower made everything still.

Then a moment like night cereus
that blooms only in the dark, waking us
with its alarm of scent.

It wasn't seeing your face so suddenly like his,
or the sight of death in her white dress;
or the glaze of summer light
hardening into crust. Not the accustomed sadness
of what we'd lost,
but a new injury, a gash
bleeding into everything:
what we were losing.

7

When there are no places left for us,
we'll still talk in order to make things true:
not only the years before we were born,
not only the names of our dead,
but also this life.
The simple feel of an apple in the hand.
The look of the table after a meal, *en déshabillé*,
rings of wine like lips staining the cloth,
the half-eaten fish in its halo of lemon and butter.
Nights of tastes, of different smoothnesses;
nights when the twister of desire touches down
and tears up sleep;
of drowning in the shadow of your own body.

But if memory is only skin,
if we become dervishes spinning
at the speed of the world, feeling
nothing,
we spend hours by the river, telling everything.
So that when we are gone, even our spirits
weighed down with stones,
the river will remember.

8

It was a suicide mission, to smuggle language
from mouths of the dying
and the dead; last words of the murdered mothers –
Germany, Poland, Russia.
They found that what they'd rescued
wasn't the old language at all;
only the alphabet the same.
Because language of a victim only reveals
the one who named him.

Because they were plucked from the centre,
because they shared the same table, same street,
there was no idiom to retreat to.

What was left but to cut out one's tongue,
or cleave it with new language,
or try to hear a language of the dead,
who were thrown into pits, into lakes –
What are the words for earth, for water?

The truth is why words fail.
We can only reveal by outline,
by circling absence.
But that's why language
can remember truth when it's not spoken.
Words in us that deafen,
that wait, even when their spell seems
wasted;
even while silence
accumulates to fate.

Prayer is the effort of wresting words
not from silence,
but from the noise of other words.
To penetrate heaven, we must reach

what breaks in us.
The image haunts me:
the double swaying
of prayer on the trains.

9

Whole cities were razed with a word.
Petersburg vanished into Leningrad, became
an invisible city where poets promised to meet
so they could pronounce again
"the blessed word with no meaning."

A writer buried his testimony
in the garden, black type in black soil,
trusting that someday earth would speak.
All those years of war and uncertainty after,
no one knew the power of his incantation,
calling quietly from its dark envelope.
From his notebook grew orchids and weeds.

Words are powerless as love,
transforming only by taking us as we are.

Reading letters from Tsvetaeva to a friend
we cried together in your barn:
"you're the only one I have left."

After all these years I still feel closest to you
in the hours reserved for nightmares,
even in our distant bedrooms.
Because I know you're awake too,
if not this night, then another,
watching your husband's sleeping body
rise with breath.

10

For years I've driven towards you in spring rain,
storm sky of green marble,
slow traffic a caravan of swinging lanterns,
windshield wipers like clock hands.
Poems by Tsvetaeva on the seat beside me,
flowers in wet paper.

As the hours pass, the hard seeds in my heart
soften and swell as I think of your kitchen
with its stone floor
like a summer house in Peredelkino,
and of Mandelstam, exiled to Yelabuga on the Kama:
"if you must leave the city,
it's best to live near a river."

You fly out of the darkness at me,
twisting open the tin sky.

The thunderstorm becomes other storms:
darkness steeping like tea above Burnside Drive,
with its slippery crease of rusted leaves;
or the night on High Street, rain
streaming like milk down the windshield
the moment the streetlights clicked on.
I think of young Akhmatova,
under a black umbrella with Modigliani,
reading Verlaine in the Luxembourg.
All the languages they spoke –
Russian, Italian, French –
and still, their lovemaking was with roses!
Language not enough
for what they had to tell each other.

Never to lose this joy,
driving to one who awaits my arrival.

Soon I will be standing on your porch, dripping
with new memory, a thin dress soaked with May rain.

Rain that helps one past grow out of another.

11

Language is the house with lamplight in its windows,
visible across fields. Approaching, you can hear
music; closer, smell
soup, bay leaves, bread — a meal for anyone
who has only his tongue left.
It's a country; home; family:
abandoned; burned down; whole lines dead, unmarried.
For those who can't read their way in the streets,
or in the gestures and faces of strangers,
language is the house to run to;
in wild nights, chased by dogs and other sounds,
when you've been lost a long time,
when you have no other place.

There are nights in the forest of words
when I panic, every step into thicker darkness,
the only way out to write myself into a clearing,
which is silence.
Nights in the forest of words
when I'm afraid we won't hear each other
over clattering branches, over
both our voices calling.

In winter, in the hour
when the sun runs liquid then freezes,
caught in the mantilla of empty trees;
when my heart listens
through the cold stethoscope of fear,
your voice in my head reminds me

what the light teaches.
Slowly you translate fear into love,
the way the moon's blood is the sea.

SUBLIMATION

Writer Alfred Doeblin, perhaps best known for his novel, *Berlin Alexanderplatz,* escaped Germany during World War II; he was one of the few exiled writers who made the difficult decision to return after the war. The poem's "shadow bride" was photographer Yolla Niclas.

A LESSON FROM THE EARTH

Johannes Kepler (1571–1630) pursued mathematical harmonies in a Europe torn by the counter-reformation and the Thirty Years War. His Three Laws freed thought by marrying astronomy and physics for the first time, paving the way directly for Newton's theory of gravity. By proving that planets follow elliptical not circular orbits, he dismantled a false and cumbersome view of the solar system, which had been tied to theology. He met and worked with Danish astronomer Tycho Brahe in 1600, a year before Tycho's death. Brahe's remarkably accurate observational data was published later in the Rudolphine Tables, named for Emperor Rudolph II, the patron of both Brahe and Kepler.

MODERSOHN – BECKER

German painter Paula Becker (1876–1907) regarded both commitments – family duty and her art – with equal seriousness; her short life was marked by a wrenching struggle between the two. She left the artists' colony of Worpswede, where she'd been living with her husband, the painter Otto Modersohn, for Paris. She returned to the marriage and later that year, at age 31, she died suddenly, shortly after giving birth to their only child.

BLUE VIGOUR

Before she became the highly acclaimed short-story writer, using the pen name Isak Dinesen, Karen Blixen emigrated from Denmark to Kenya, where she ran a farm from 1913 to 1931. Her love and respect for the land and its people are documented in her paintings and memoirs.

STONE

Lunia Czechowska, a Russian émigré, met the Italian painter Amedeo Modigliani in Paris in 1917, three years before his death. At the time, Modigliani was living with the painter Jeanne Hébuterne.

WHAT THE LIGHT TEACHES

Marina Tsvetaeva, Osip Mandelstam, and Anna Akhmatova – three of Russia's best known modern poets – all suffered under Stalinist repression. While exiled in France, Tsvetaeva endured terrible personal hardship, as is revealed in her letters.

ACKNOWLEDGEMENTS

"The source of love becomes the object of love."
– Joseph Brodsky

"Miner's Pond" is for Howard, Arlen, and Martin; Rosalind and Isaiah Michaels.

"What The Light Teaches" is for Janis Freedman.

"Fresh Mint" is for Vivian Palin.

Special thanks to Sam Solecki for his editorial guidance. And to Linda Williams for guiding this book into print.

Thanks to Christopher Dewdney, for longstanding support. Thanks to Jeff and Janis, Arlene and Anne, Gord and Roz, Charles and Richard, Luigi and Nan, Ted and George.

Thanks to the editors of the magazines where some of these poems first appeared: *Saturday Night, The Malahat Review,* and *What* magazine.

The brief quotations that appear in "Miner's Pond" are from John Noble Wilford's *The Riddle of the Dinosaur* (Alfred Knopf); John McLoughlin's *Synapsida: A New Look into the Origin of Mammals* (Viking Press); and Timothy Ferris's *Coming of Age in the Milky Way* (William Morrow). "Pillar Of Fire" is based on the log entries of Captain Watson, of the H.M.S. *Charles Bal.*

The generous assistance of the Ontario Arts Council and the Woodcock Fund is gratefully acknowledged.